**What's being said about
'HEARTSPACE – Letters To My Mother'**

"Jude's writing is directly from the heart. Her new book, 'Heartspace – Letters To My Mother' is full of raw emotion, honesty and vulnerability. Jude gives us all permission to fully connect with, embrace and express all aspects of loss, grief and coming to terms with losing a loved one. Her first book has touched lives around the world and I have no doubt that this will do the same."
Alison Burton, Director - Simply Natural Therapies

"... Judy lives the reality that death is not the end, that love and a relationship are much stronger than death. Her heartfelt letters to her mother offer a clear insight into the power of this Love. By sharing this journey others will gain strength and confidence to grow their relationship with their loved ones."
Glen Lord, President - The Grief Toolbox,
President - Compassionate Friends USA

"Judy Taylor is a beautiful example of living from the heart, not the head. Her messages spread light around the world. What a true blessing ... I love it! Very raw and honest. Very, very powerful. I think that is what the world needs....authenticity."
Lynda Cheldelin Fell, President - National Grief & Hope Coalition
Creator – Grief Diaries

"... The focus is less on dwelling on loss and more on living a full and meaningful life. Lessons we learn from our deceased loved ones are priceless in showing us how to live in the moment and be truly present. It's to Judy's credit that she opens her heart so that we can heal ours."
Rose Inserra, Best Selling author - 'Dictionary of Dreams'

"HEARTSPACE – Letters To My Mother' reveals that through letter-writing to a loved one, our heartfelt emotions can be expressed in a healthy and healing way. It beautifully shows that our connections never have to end and our relationships can even become closer."
Christine Duminiak, Certified Grief Recovery Specialist
Author - Grammy Visits From Heaven

**Also by Judy Taylor
'MUM MOMENTS - Journey Through Grief"**

"... I bought this book on Amazon and loved it so much that I bought the hard copy too - it really helped me after losing my dad and I passed it on to my mum who has said it has greatly helped her too. I can't recommend this book highly enough for anyone who has lost a loved one."
Trudy Brookes - Rainbow Rays Reiki

"I love your story and your true honesty and rawness. It speaks deep from within your soul."
Angela Cartwright (President National Grief Awareness)

"I highly recommend it!! Just finished it last night! Amazing and touching!"
Robin Winsor

"I LOVE this book. It has helped me tremendously and continues to help me. For anyone going through grief I would highly recommend it... It's a long road, and I miss (my parents) so much. Sometimes there are just no words"
Doris Pelletier Jarvis

"I have just been reading your book and so many things you write hit home. I lost my mum suddenly last year (she was 62) she died unexpectedly ... I never got to say goodbye to her... Thank you for your journey and sharing it with others, Judy"
Sara Amos

"I was at Judy Taylor's book launch last year... I lost my mum just on 12 months ago. I only just recently picked up Jude's book to read. I laughed, cried and could relate to her story in so many ways... I am blessed to have met you and share your journey. You are an inspiration..."
Annalisa Seville

"Thank you the tears I have being trying to hide are flowing freely after reading nearly half of your beautiful book I look forward to finding peace in writing to my mum thanks it is a big help xx"
Hayley Comley

"Jude, while reading your book I feel so connected with my Mom. Spirituality lifted... Truly Amazing! Thank you for sharing your Journey!.. Just what I need! God Bless XO"
Erin Piotroski-Olshefski

"I thoroughly enjoyed reading Mum Moments. Having lost my mom unexpectedly last November, so much of what Judy wrote really hit home. I know that I will read it multiple times as I continue on my own journey through the unspeakable grief that comes from suddenly losing my mom and best friend."
Denise Fleming (Kindle edition)

HEARTSPACE
Letters To My Mother

Judy Taylor

Copyright © 2016 Judy Taylor

All rights reserved. This book or any portion thereof may not be reproduced or used in any manner whatsoever without the express written permission of the publisher except for the use of brief quotations in a book review or scholarly journal.

First Published by Positive Signs 2016
www.positivesigns.com.au
posigns@bigpond.net.au

Author: Judy Taylor
Cover, Edit & Layout: John Taylor

Judy Taylor has asserted her right under the Copyright, Designs and Patents Act 1988 to be identified as the author of this work. The information in this book is based on the author's experiences and opinions. The publisher specifically disclaims responsibility for any adverse consequences which may result from use of the information contained herein.

Paperback printed Internationally through Ingram Spark and distributed through Lightning Source

ISBN (Paperback): 978-0-9924900-3-4
ISBN (Ebook): 978-0-9924900-4-1

For details contact the publisher at the above email address.

HEARTSPACE
Letters To My Mother

Judy Taylor

Love Transcends Death

INTRODUCTION

by John Taylor

Death is an ending but also a new beginning.

When her mother died suddenly and unexpectedly in February 2011 Judy started writing a grief journal. She didn't think of it as that at the time but she quickly found that putting her feelings down on paper helped her cope with the grief that, at times, 'threatened to overwhelm her'. Her writing became a way she could freely express her feelings and quickly became her personal healing tool.

If you have already read Jude's first book, 'MUM MOMENTS – Journey Through Grief' which was compiled from those journals then you know Jude has an ability to express raw, honest emotions. Feelings around grief and loss don't just end and she found a way to express herself that also provided comfort and support to others. Anyone who has experienced grief knows it can feel very lonely at times. Knowing you are not alone can be powerfully therapeutic.

Jude kept writing and her writing evolved with her grief. Time does heal and much of that healing is personal growth. We all evolve. Often her writing took the form of a conversation with her mother that had nothing to do with grief. They have all been assembled here in the form of letters; what they would have talked about in any mother-daughter chat.

Judy's words continue to inspire and assist so many people everywhere and we are grateful for the overwhelmingly positive feedback. To genuinely help people in need is a wonderful and satisfying occupation.

We sincerely hope you enjoy 'Heartspace – Letters To My Mother' and that Judy's honest expression of thoughts and feelings will be of benefit to you in some way as you continue your own personal journey.

John Taylor

July 2015

14th April 2015

This morning I wrote a letter to my mum. I was sharing my feelings with her. She listened without comment or judgement allowing me to express myself freely.

I was able to process my feelings and choose my next step. Writing is a wonderful healing tool.

This is my letter:

Mum,

I've been wanting to feel your presence more lately and it feels like you are slipping away. I'm so lonely for your touch, for your guidance, for you to be here.

Even when you were here, we weren't in each other's pocket. There was a presence, a knowing that you were here. We often acknowledged we both needed still time away from family and friends, just to be with ourselves. Sometimes that was for a short time and sometimes longer.

Sometimes we found it extremely difficult to communicate with each other and other times we were totally in tune.

Right now I am extremely challenged as I step outside myself to create and develop projects to help and support me, my family and fellow human beings.

I know I'm on the right path. However my conditioning and patterns are stepping in big time. I feel like I have to fight every step of the way.

Well that's not totally true. Sometimes I feel I'm in tune with my journey and my heart sings as I take one step at a time. Other times I just want everything in place right now and for everything to be okay and then I remember everything is okay no matter what is happening.

Life has a purpose and when I accept that everything that happens to us leads us in the direction we need to go it will make it easier for me.

I love you mum,

**Back in 2013, following the completion of
'Mum Moments – Journey Through Grief'
Judy wrote...**

Mum,

As I sit and ponder I had the epiphany that my Mum Moments book is ready to go out into the big wide world and I'm excited. I'm excited for me and I'm excited for all the people that are going to read it. I know it has assisted me on my journey since your death and I hope it will assist others as they take their own journey through death and grieving.

I am so happy that I have written this for me, shared it with and for you Mum, and sharing it with others who take comfort in self-expression.

Who would have thought that I would find my shining light through your loss? You always knew there was a spark inside of me ready to shine. I hope my shining light is of benefit to all who read my book (journal)

20 years ago I wrote:

> "Through vulnerability comes inner strength."

- - - - - - -

Mum,

Today I wrote these words:

'Love that resonates from the heart is love in any language'

'The Heart's Intuitive Intelligence'

'The 'HEARTSPACE is very powerful'

- - - - - - -

Mum,

I have these moments when I have a clear vision of you and realise you are just not here anymore.

It's hard to believe that you are no longer alive on planet earth when your presence with me is so strong.

Everything that resonated in the past with you still resonates now.

Death cannot take you away from me.

Our love spreads way beyond live on earth.

- - - - - - -

> Being 'in the moment' is the gift that will lead you into the future.

Mum,

I now know that the pain of losing you is exacerbated by the pain of the conflict in our maternal family. The perceptions created by each one of us are not true and highlight the power of the ego on planet earth.

Wishing for peace means it is not here. Creating inner peace brings me home to a place where I can share my peace too.

The pain in my heart for the family I grew up with needs to be loved and nurtured everyday. It may not be real but it hurts.

I need to ask for hugs to get through the pain.

I will feel the love as I hug the pain.

Miss you

- - - - - - -

Sometimes a Mother is the best person to talk to.

Sometimes the only way is face to face.

When that is no longer an option then sometimes it's hard.

I miss your physical presence on planet earth, Mum.

Love you.

Mum,

Through writing my feelings after your loss I have found me. Your death has given me the greatest gift a mother can give - the gift of love, the gift of understanding and the gift of knowing myself.

As my journey continues since your death it feels I have experienced every emotion known to mankind. My journal writing has sustained me through the times when I have felt totally connected with you on a spiritual level and the most unbearable and painful times when the physical loss has been so excruciatingly painful that I thought I would never get over the pain.

It's not quite 3 years since you died – you are ever present with me and I know your love for me has no boundaries.

- - - - - - -

Mum,

I am adventuring into the most powerful time in my life and I'm scared.

Well, my ego is scared.

I'm just getting 'yes, yes, yes' and it feels so good, it feels so powerful and it feels so right.

My intuition is so strong, so resilient, so right and my ego is so frightened, so scared and unsure.

My ego needs validation and is challenging my intuition every step of the way.

I need to listen to my intuition, understand my ego, validate my ego, love my ego, thank my ego for protecting me and follow my intuitive guidance.

Each day stillness is a priority for me as I allow my intuition and ego to work together for the benefit of my highest good and the highest good of all concerned.

I love myself. Love is good.

- - - - - - -

Mum,

Today I start living in the moment listening to my intuition. I have stopped my paid work and plan to spend my time releasing my first book - a journal we will call 'Mum Moments - Journey Through Grief'.

I have been guided for the last 3 months to let go of working for someone else and work for me, trusting that 'Mum Moments' is my journey home to me.

My ego has been stepping in all my life to protect me from perceived dangers and assisting me to make decisions that are 'right', whatever that means. The chatter in my head has supported me successfully up till now, however it no longer works for me.

I am going to share space with all the voices in my head over the days and months ahead as I forge forward with my true destiny in mind.

Writing is a gift I have experienced all my life, my true way to communicate with the world, to assist myself and others. Through my willingness to know me and understand me I have been able to support myself and others on their own journey.

Many a time I have been in tune with my pathway and many a time I have allowed my ego rather than my heart and intuition to guide me.

I know my heart and intuition are the true essence of me and the joy I feel when I acknowledge this is exponential.

'Self-expression is the key.'

- - - - - - -

Mum,

I shared many Mum Moments with you. We did so many things together over the years.

Now I find watching any Mother-Daughter movies really touches a sensitive spot.

Miss you mum.

- - - - - - -

Mum,

Yesterday the moment has passed.

Today in the moment I'm enjoying being me.

- - - - - - -

My intuition is guiding me today.

Baby steps ...

I know what this means for me.

Listening to my intuition brings me into the present moment.

I'm scared … scared of fear itself.

The feeling that I'm so close to realising my dream and so far from taking the final steps.

Why, I don't know.

I'm so excited but something inside of me, my ego, is holding me, wanting me to turn around and take the easy path, whatever that is.

I feel like a part of me is scared and doesn't want to go there…

Go where?

On this journey into me

The 'me' that feels like me

That 'me' that has so much to share, so much to offer and so much love

So what's stopping me?

Mum,

My challenge…

Stay in the moment.

Step by Step.

I am grateful for this process on my publishing journey.

I heard you say:

'Give yourself the gift of stillness. Tune in to your intuition and listen to your inner knowing. There you will find the best guidance for you.'

- - - - - - -

Mum,

I know I'm on the right pathway when I consistently have whoopee feelings in my day.

A saying I came up with approximately 20 years ago that still resonates for me today:

'Through Vulnerability comes
Inner Strength'.

I'm in full flight, Mumma … I'm blooming.

- - - - - - -

Mum,

As I close my eyes and allow the breeze to flow through me I am at peace in this moment and all is ok. I am invincible, I'm me and I am perfect.

Whatever choices I make following this moment will be the best choice for me and all that surrounds me.

Then I heard you say:

'Slow down, take a breath and then move on. The importance of what lies ahead for you is not relevant right now. Just know if you ground yourself, slow down and take a breath the world will be at peace within you.

You create a better world for yourself and everyone that comes into your world. Your gift is to be yourself, listen to your intuition and let the world flow.

Amazing things will unfold just because you believe. Take the work out of it, live it, breathe it, love it and everyone will benefit.'

In that moment I felt all is well. The overwhelm I often feel is okay too. Being alive is a beautiful feeling. Just let go, take the need to always be in control out of life and allow the flow.

Whoa ...

I'm feeling like I'm moving into a new dimension. I need to sit and allow my being to absorb what's unfolding. My intent is right for me in the given moment and all will be taken care of.

I will be presented with all that I need for me to be fully present in the moment and the abundance necessary for my life will be provided in ways I could never have imagined.

Everything is perfect in the given moment.

> Reach out for your Dreams ...
> they are there waiting for you

- - - - - - -

Mum,

I'm sitting in front of a fan on this hot summer day just trying to 'be'.

Well, actually I'm allowing myself to be in the moment.

I write in the moment, I feel in the moment, and in this moment I write exactly what's coming through me.

- - - - - - -

Mum,

Whoa ... I'm scared, I believe in this, I'm not used to living this, I'm being blown away by all I'm being given. Take a breath, little by little, step by step, baby steps.

I know everything happens in good time. So I tune in and I write... I tune out for a while. Every day there are words for me and I feel so many are important lessons to write. I feel already that they will be the ones that can help everyone on a daily basis.

Most times it's about trust.

It's simple: I believe, I move forward by listening to my intuition and letting it guide me every step of the way.

I try to share love wherever I go.

Let Your Light Shine From Within.

Jude xoxoxo

- - - - - - -

Mum,

I'm scared - no I'm not.

I'm on a roller coaster - the words keep coming. What do I do with them? Take a breath.

Whoa...

- - - - - - -

Mum,

I love the feeling when you hold a book and you feel the power within.

Sometimes you need to read the whole book.

Sometimes you need to focus on the thought: 'what do I need right now?' while holding on to the book... and the answer presents.

> The lessons I teach are the lessons I practice.
>
> Positive intent provides positive results.

Mum,

I moved out of home when I needed you most.

I was married at 19.

My daughter is now 19 and I am finding this time with her one of the most valuable. At 19 I ran away from this valuable connection and that's okay because I found my own Mum in me.

I celebrate growing older.

I celebrate the wisdom I bring with age.

I celebrate the benefit I receive from knowing me.

I celebrate the moment as I age gracefully.

I am grateful for age.

Mum,

Yesterday I had all these words coming through me. I thought I would take them all in and write it all down later. Today, I know that 'in the moment' is the right time to write them, that's when they resonate.

The words just come. They flow through me with ease. 'In the moment' is when I need to write them down.

I've been screaming out to be heard all my life. Now I'm hearing me.

You gave me the gift of life at birth.

At death you have given me the gift of life again.

Jude xoxoxo

- - - - - - -

Mum,

I am learning that on the mother-daughter journey sometimes we need to sit back, be there in silence, observe and offer support. If we see something we feel we want to show or teach our daughter then it's usually a lesson for us as well. If we practise living authentically ourselves then our daughters will pick it up.

Having experienced being a teenage daughter myself and having a 19 year old daughter of my own I recognise that sometimes we need to disconnect for a while in order to strengthen our connection.

Room to grow.

Mum,

This came to me this morning:

'Intuitive guidance'

When someone asks you a question or when you ask yourself a question the intuitive answer is within you before the question is finished.

So I ask:

'Are you willing to start listening to your intuition today?

Are you willing to practise listening to your intuition every day?'

Live intuitively.

Right Brain - left brain working together.

- - - - - - -

You know the moment.

That's the moment.

The time when you are supposed to share.

This is it.

- - - - - - -

Mum,

Some of my thoughts today:

'You have been taking care of things for so long. Now you are taking care of yourself, everything is taken care of. Trust in the process everything is perfect. Love is the answer.'

'Remember in any given moment we can be aware of patterns in our life that work for us and patterns that no longer work for us. In the moment we can choose to change the patterns.'

'Your enthusiasm takes over sometimes - listen to your intuition - that's where you will find your power. Intuitively you shine - shine now.'

'Today I celebrate knowing the moments I can learn from.'

'There's no need to explain me - just be me.'

'I'm celebrating being aware that I'm having a challenging day and my enthusiasm can jump ahead of my intuition. As the day unfolds I'm practicing listening to my intuition in the moment.'

'Self-expression brings you home to you.'

'Create … it's your destiny.'

- - - - - - -

Mum,

I feel like I'm being challenged to go somewhere, to a particular place just to see if I'm willing to listen. Then, once I'm there, I'm being told I can leave …

'Yes, you are listening.'

Where to next?

'You already have the answer.'

Thank you.

- - - - - - -

Practise Grace whatever that means for you.

- - - - - - -

Mum,

I just read this in my Mum Moments journal …

'As I sit quietly in the early hours with the light of a burning candle, I realise your light continues to shine in my life…'

It still touches me.

Love Jude

- - - - - - -

Mum,

3 years ... I remember your last breath as you ascended to a place unknown.

I began an unknown journey too. A journey of twists and turns, experiencing unbelievable pain and exhilarating joy as I discovered a different way to connect with you.

I thank you for guiding me every step of the way in life and now in death.

I love you Mum

- - - - - - -

Mum,

In a shop today a lady said: "I always buy clothes and when I get them home I don't like them. I can't make decisions."

I asked her if she was aware of what she was saying and repeated it back to her. I suggested that she had a choice to change her wording and buy clothes that she will like when she gets home.

The example I gave her was:

I buy clothes that I feel comfortable in. I make decisions that work for me.

Then I asked her:

Do you want to change the patterns in your life?

Her immediate response was "No".

I said, "That's okay - it's great to know you have a choice."

Self Awareness is the key to making choices that work for you.

- - - - - - -

Happy Anniversary ... your journey home.

- - - - - - -

Hi Mum,

Sometimes I'm not too sure and then I feel totally connected. I realise a willingness *not* to know is actually a willingness *to* know. It's amazing how words can have meanings depending on how you are feeling.

It's beautiful to know we can choose our own destiny.

I love you Mum.

- - - - - - -

Mum,

As the day comes to an end I have enjoyed some Mum Moments and other times just being in the moment. Who knows what will unfold in any given moment?

As the day comes to an end a new day begins.

Life ...

- - - - - - -

Mum,

So many thoughts today ...

Sometimes filling in time just feels like filling in time. Not sure if I want to go there, not sure if I want to be there.

I would much rather be in the moment, experiencing the moment, living in the moment. Living in the moment is where I want to be. Living in the moment is where I am me.

My journey to now is perfect for where I am right now.

I heard you say:

'Now is exactly how it's meant to be. Live now and the journey into the future will take care of itself.'

My intent is to help and support myself and others.

'Value yourself and the gifts you have and share for the benefit of all.

'You know your story. You know your journey. You know what helped you along the way. Others have experienced similar journeys. Help others appreciate and value their journey by sharing your story. We are one.'

> 'When I focus on the destination it's easy to miss the journey.
>
> When I focus on the journey the destination unfolds'.

Hi Mum,

These came to me today:

'When your intent is to help and support yourself and others then you radiate positive energy that touches people in amazing ways.'

'Love yourself and share the love and watch love radiate.'

'When you feel the attraction take action.'

'Today I am making a difference one step at a time.'

- - - - - - -

Mum,

All feelings have a purpose. When we embrace all our feelings without judgement we have a choice to release unresolved feelings from the past. Feelings offer healings.

Healing begins when we embrace our feelings.

- - - - - - -

Mum,

Some thoughts from my day:

'I practise nurturing myself, taking care of me, loving myself and being in the moment. When I do this I am able to support others on their journey and life is good.'

'Simplicity ... Live in the Moment.'

'I'm being guided every step of the way. I'm listening.'

'I am grateful for every moment.'

> May self-awareness be your key
> to the joy of life

- - - - - - -

Mum,

I have something very special I am going to release to the world shortly.

Special because it represents who I am and the power of healing through our willingness to be vulnerable.

My journey shows through vulnerability we find our inner strength.

I look forward to sharing.

- - - - - - -

Mum,

More thoughts from my day. They keep coming so I keep writing them down.

'Take a moment to be still with your loved ones and they will be right beside you wherever they are.'

'The perfect moment is now.'

'Sometimes it's the little things that make a difference.'

- - - - - - -

Mum,

In the moment as I ponder the next step on my project I am feeling uncertain of the direction.

Intuitively I get to change my earrings which I have been wearing for a long time. So I do it and something shifted.

Now I feel ready for the next step.

I am reminded to listen to the signs I am given. They are there to help me.

In the moment of patience ... opportunities present.

Today I have been given the opportunity to practise patience several times. It is apparent I need to practise patience.

lol ...

- - - - - - -

Mum,

Today's word: 'Celebrate'

May everyone do something today that gives them that awesome feeling of Celebration.

At this awesome point please take a moment to be still and feel the Celebration in your heart.

Doing it takes practise. The more I practise doing it the easier it gets. Each step presents the next step. Some are easier than others, some take more practise.

As I keep doing it I am presented with the next step.

One step at a time.

- - - - - - -

In any given moment I can make a choice that works best for me.

In any given moment you can make a choice that works best for you.

There is a Positive Sign in every experience.

- - - - - - -

Mum,

I am acknowledging the gifts I have to help and support myself and others.

I am grateful a friend called me this morning. I listened, I heard, I offered support to help her tune in to her intuition and guided her as she listened to her own inner knowing.

At the end of the conversation she said "I felt like a 2 out of 10 when I rang you. Now I feel 10 out of 10."

For me she had chosen to embrace her whole self from a space of love.

We all have the answers within ourselves. In any given moment we have the choice to listen to our Inner Knowing.

Love you

- - - - - - -

Mum,

Taking it easy - gentle on me. I am at an exciting turning point in my life and some of my old patterns are screaming to be heard as I change direction.

It is important to acknowledge these patterns as they have been serving a purpose for many years. There is a saying, 'what you resist persists'.

If you allow your feelings to present without judgement and observe rather than resist, then you have a choice to change your reaction.

Mum,

At 2:00am this morning I was awake and in a state of stress. I lay back and asked the question, "What's the feeling? Where is it coming from?"

I listened, I got answers, I embraced the feelings without judgement.

I acknowledged the feelings and I observed my feelings of wanting to run away from it all. The fear … I was so scared. I felt it, I watched it, I didn't try to get rid of it and somehow I fell asleep.

Next thing I know I'm waking up feeling totally confident that I'm on the right track and all is well.

- - - - - - -

'Stillness is the space where
healing begins'

- - - - - - -

Mum,

I want to write an 'I'm feeling' book.

When we get in touch with our feelings we have an opportunity to choose what we do with those feelings.

That wonderful feeling when you allow yourself to have a treat of some kind:

Bed - relax, meditate, glide into your day

Shower - feel the warmth of the water, like a waterfall, cleanse your body, massage, feel …

Mum,

I am lighting a candle for me and lighting a candle for others.

My journal has been an amazing healing tool for me and I trust my vision to share it with others for their benefit will provide a healing tool for all.

I sat under the shower and visualised myself under a waterfall.

It was a beautiful experience for me.

- - - - - - -

When you feel like you are
being slowed down, it's a great
chance to practise patience.

- - - - - - -

Mum,

As I take one step at a time it is amazing how opportunities present to guide me to the next step.

- - - - - - -

When your life suddenly changes forever, the only option is to live in the moment and value each step.

- - - - - - -

Hi Mum,

My intuition says 'STOP'.

What's that mean, I ask?

'STOP trying to fix everything. Take care of what you know is important right now. Let the rest be taken care of itself.'

'Be still, listen, be guided by your inner knowing. The answers are there. It's time to trust.'

It feels so good when I do this. The love I feel is amazing.

Love you

- - - - - - -

I know I'm on the right track because my ego is challenging me every step of the way.

I will remember to trust and listen to my intuition.

- - - - - - -

Mum,

Letter to a facebook friend:

'My ego is crying out to be heard. I am being challenged every step of the way. When all my past patterns say: 'Jude's the one who can make it happen for you … If you want someone to fix it, Jude's the one'.

Spirit is saying, 'one step at a time, you don't have to make it all happen right now.'

When I listen to Spirit then the answers come to me.

- - - - - - -

Mum,

I have found stillness is a beautiful place to grieve. In the stillness I come home to my heart and allow the healing process to present.

- - - - - - -

Mum,

I wrote this to a friend on facebook today:

'I am sorry for your loss - I trust you have allowed yourself to grieve when the feelings surface.

'Alone is an interesting word. When we are alone we experience different emotions. We can label them as positive or negative feelings or we can just be with them and observe what unfolds.

'Sometimes I find being alone uncomfortable and others times I love it. Being a mother, having time alone is wonderful.'

- - - - - - -

Mum,

The more I live me, acknowledging any judgements I feel and choosing to be me anyway, the happier I feel.

I recommend to everyone to practise living your own truth. The more you practise, the more it resonates.

- - - - - - -

Questions I find myself asking more and more:

Did you know that being still, listening to your intuition and being guided by your inner knowing will guide you to your next step?

Are you willing to practise this in your daily life?

I help people get to know themselves so they can make choices that work for them.

- - - - - - -

Mum,

Many years ago when I was doing my Diploma of Holistic Healing I remembered on the way in that one of my friends from the course was having a birthday. I stopped in a small shopping strip to buy her a gift and realised I only had a small amount of cash with me. I put out the intent to find the right gift for her and got 'buy her a whole pumpkin' as I walked towards a gift shop. So I bought a pumpkin for her.

When I gave her the pumpkin - she said 'do you know what pumpkins represent?'

I said no.

She said 'Pumpkins represent Abundance' and gave me the biggest thank you hug.

Listen to your intuition.

- - - - - - -

Mum,

Sometimes it is easy to be with you in Spirit sometimes it's not.

Sometimes I'd like to give you a big hug and feel the power of touch.

Sometimes it's easy to love you the way it is.

Sometimes it takes my breath away.

Love you

- - - - - - -

Mum,

Yesterday I drank my green juice.

However, today when I sat on the front porch sipping on my green juice I *really tasted it*. I tuned in and enjoyed the flavour of each mouthful.

I wiped my finger inside the glass to get all the froth around the edges.

I was aware of the goodness going into my body.

When I take a moment to nurture myself I feel good.

Mum,

Message for me today:

Each step I take is a step closer to my destination.

As I take these steps, I embrace all of me, the comfortable and uncomfortable feelings. I celebrate being me.

Each step I take is the step closer to my destination.

Jude

- - - - - - -

'The more I listen to my intuition, the more I am guided in the right direction'

- - - - - - -

Message to me:

Whatever we do we are going to have so much fun doing it.

- - - - - - -

Mum,

When nurturing myself is my number one priority everything else falls into place for me.

When everything is not falling into place it's a reminder to nurture myself.

'There is no recipe for grieving.
In any given moment the
feelings come and go

Live in the moment'

- - - - - - -

Mum,

Today I am taking my own advice and living in the moment.

I enjoyed my lunch on the front porch soaking up the sunshine.

Chicken, avocado, cucumber, sprouts and lettuce sandwich.

Enjoying each individual mouthful.

Yum …

- - - - - - -

Mum,

When I injure myself I take the opportunity to reflect on where I am right now and any other conscious beliefs that are presenting in my life.

In the moment I can make a choice on the healing process that works for me on physical, mental and spiritual levels.

- - - - - - -

Mum,

I observe the moments that bring a smile to my face and observe the ones that don't.

Each moment has a purpose.

In the stillness the purpose will present.

Mum,

I have found my way.

It may not be everybody's way.

It's my way and it works for me.

When I live my way, my Spirit sings.

May everyone experience the way to get their Spirit singing.

Jude

Mum,

Our willingness to embrace our self-awareness is uplifting.

Embracing ourselves without judgement and making choices that work for us is empowering.

The emotions we experience along the way all have a purpose.

Mum,

I remind myself to breathe. It's so close I can taste it. The nerves keep surfacing and I keep breathing.

Mum,

In a place of stillness you discover who you really are.

You also discover the inner voices that prevent you from standing in your own power.

This is a positive sign because in this space you have a choice to be you.

Mum,

Today I'm thinking about the fact that I am one of five girls. I know that each of my sisters experienced their own relationship with you when you were alive.

At times I have been surprised and felt hurt by some of our perceptions. I found being true to my own feelings and voicing them has helped me get through.

I understand that any sad event triggers emotions we then move through, and I know how much I suffered through the experience of your dying. We each did it in our own way.

Grief is a personal experience which brings out so many different responses and reactions.

Mum,

I just looked out the window and embraced the magic of the awesome colours. These are moments that can make a difference.

Jude

Mum,

I understand me

I help people understand themselves

I listen to me

I help people practise listening to themselves

I choose what is best for me

I help people make choices that are best for them.

Jude

Mum,

One thing is for sure, we are all surrounded by our mother's love. The connection between mother and daughter never dies.

I know the physical loss can be unbearable at times. However I know you are always with me in Spirit.

Love you,

Mum,

I write to help and support myself. I love to write all my feelings without judgement.

I start with 'I'm feeling…' and just let it rip until I come to a space of peace and calm understanding.

Sometimes I keep what I write. Sometimes I don't.

I find writing is a supportive health and healing tool for me.

I know that feeling.

I know that moment.

It's the 'I'll call mum' moment.

Miss you

My mum was 78 when she died. One moment she was dancing with me at my husband's 60th birthday celebration and the next she left the dance floor and had a massive stroke.

I personally, and many others, experienced her as the youngest 78-year-old woman we had ever met.

In my good moments I celebrate that her last moments were an expression of her love of dancing. In the toughest moments I just want her right beside me in this physical life again.

Right here and now, in this moment, I can feel her beside me on our new journey together.

The emotions come and go.

Mum,

Grieving is such a personal experience. Sometimes it raises some resistance. Other times it surfaces in so many different ways.

Everyone is different.

I found that allowing myself to experience my own feelings worked for me. Everyone has to find their own way.

Writing my feelings supported me on my journey. Writing gave me permission to feel.

Mum,

Today on my Mum Moments facebook page some people shared their beautiful and sad stories with me. All I could do was reply...

'I feel deeply for you all. I was 55 when my mum died three years ago.

Many a time through my grieving I have felt like a two year old as I cried out, "I want my mummy and I want her now".

She was 78 and I was 55, however the mother-child connection from childhood is as powerful today as when I was two years old.'

- - - - - - -

Mum,

Giving yourself permission to feel is the greatest gift you can give yourself. Owning your feelings and allowing yourself to feel them with your own child teaches them that it is okay to have feelings.

It can be as simple as 'sometimes I miss my Mum and it feels so sad that I cry'.

Your child then learns that it is okay to express their feelings too. The magic words here to start with are "I feel ..."

- - - - - - -

Mum,

It constantly surprises me how, through my willingness to be vulnerable, I find my inner strength.

- - - - - - -

Mum,

This morning I woke from a dream where I was crying for the feeling of death. It was deep. It was raw. It was real.

I lay in bed allowing myself the conscious time to be. I came to a place where these words came to me.

> 'Stillness is a place where I give myself permission to feel.
>
> I open my heart and find myself.
>
> I help people to open their heart and find themselves.'

- - - - - - -

Mum,

I find sometimes it is important to stop, observe and take one step at a time. Stillness is a place where you have a clear vision of what is happening for you. The choices I make from this space are profound.

So the question is:

'Do you ever have those moments when you get 'Stop'?

I do. When I stop I am amazed by the experience of the moment. I recommend embracing the moment as a positive sign on your wellness journey.

Jude

- - - - - - -

Mum,

Today's words:

'In this moment you have the choice to change the direction of your life'

'Practising stillness and patience today ... one step at a time'

'Receiving and sending the essence of love from all directions'

'Write the words ... the words will be read

Write from the heart ... the words will heal

Write from a space of love ... the words will unfold

Write from a space of pain ... the words will heal.'

I feel like I'm in a trance the words keep coming.

'Stay grounded'

Jude

- - - - - - -

Mum,

When I allow all my feelings to flow I come to a space of love.

Feelings come and go just like waves. Feelings are a positive sign in any given moment.

Feelings are here for everyone to observe and embrace and choose how to react.

- - - - - - -

Mum,

I am ready for the roller coaster ride of life. I have no idea where it's going. I'm in it for the adventure. In the moment I'm loving it.

- - - - - - -

Mum,

You are there with me every step of the way through the highs, lows and in-betweens.

You communicate with me whenever I am willing to be with you and hear you.

I know I am surrounded by your love.

Jude

- - - - - - -

Mum,

I continue to write and today I wrote this:

'Since my Mum's death in 2011 writing has been my saviour, my healing tool.

My writing has brought me home to me and allowed me to continue my connection with my Mum.

These are my words right now. This is my expression of me on my journey.'

Later:

'I'm watching a movie and it's there. It's a feeling. It's my Mum and it's real. I can feel her. She's here, right here beside me. I can feel the emotion. I can feel the tears. She's right here beside me.

It's different now.'

- - - - - - -

Mum,

Abundance presents in amazing ways.

I was offered some garden mulch earlier in the week so we embraced the opportunity.

The weather forecast all week has been rain, rain, rain however the universe has provided sunshine, sunshine, sunshine.

Sometimes when an opportunity presents it's time to change your plans and be spontaneous.

Mum,

My Act of self Love is to practise stillness and patience.

There's a part of me just wants to scream out to the world.

'Here it is, a healing space.'

In the stillness, I am being guided.

'Trust, divine timing' is my message.

Believing, knowing, trusting ...

Mum,

As I look out the window more than 3 years after your death, I realise how the mother-daughter connection lives forever.

I feel I have experienced every emotion known to mankind on this journey. And, as in life as in death you have been right beside me every step of the way.

I love you Mum

Mum,

I am celebrating ...

Writing my journal

Believing in my vision

Trusting the process

Embracing my self-publishing journey

Creating my Facebook page

Creating my website

Printing my journal

One of the best parts of this journey has been sharing this experience with my husband John. Our complimentary skills have brought us to a beautiful space in our life and our work.

I look forward to sharing my story with everyone who will benefit from my words.

Jude

- - - - - - -

Mum,

At your funeral I had a journal with me and asked people to write a memory of you.

I treasure it.

- - - - - - -

Mum,

The physical loss is a shocker.

I have found in the stillness of the moment I can often feel you right here beside me. It may be sitting in the garden thinking of you and a butterfly flies past. It might be a song you love that comes on the radio or the warmth of a shawl you gave me.

I feel your presence in so many ways and it supports me.

I love you Mum.

- - - - - - -

Mum,

To everyone who has lost their mother I say:

'May you feel the presence of your Mum in everything you do today.

I often go to a cafe or a special place I shared with my Mum to be with her, feel her and love her.

I find I have great experiences when I do this… fun, laughter and tears.'

Thank you Mum for everything.

- - - - - - -

Mum,

I wrote this today:

Remember ...

Every step you take brings you closer to your destination. Every destination brings you to another journey.

Take a moment to enjoy each step.

Jude

- - - - - - -

Hi Mum,

For me personal development is a gift you give to yourself that radiates from within and shines like the sunshine.

Written from the heart ...

- - - - - - -

Mum,

I will be celebrating all that you mean to me on Mother's Day. We experienced every emotion together on the roller coaster of life.

Jude

- - - - - - -

Mum,

I practise celebrating you every day.

Some days it feels like 3 days ago rather than 3 years since you died.

Sometimes the pain is deep.

Sometimes the joy of your presence in my life before death is wonderful.

Sometimes I feel your presence in my life after death is so powerful.

I often feel surrounded by your love.

- - - - - - -

Mum,

On my facebook page today I said to someone grieving:

'Do whatever helps.

You find your own healing tools along the way.

I often go to places my mum and I enjoyed together and allow the emotion of the moment.

I feel so close to my mum at these times.'

- - - - - - -

The more I allow my emotions,
the more I feel love in my
heart.

Hi Mum,

From the moment of conception we are connected forever.

In death the connection is still there, it's just different.

- - - - - - -

Mum,

When we grieve people often stand back because they don't know what to say. Allowing yourself to feel gives other people permission to experience their feelings too.

Most importantly my healing has come by allowing myself to be me. Crying when I feel like crying. Laughing when I feel like laughing.

Love and hugs to everyone grieving.

- - - - - - -

Mum,

Sometimes I feel like an excited child with the anticipation of Easter or Christmas.

When you died you left me with a gift. Your gift was self expression through writing.

- - - - - - -

Mum,

As I sit peacefully in Cavallini Cafe in Clifton Hill I am giving myself permission to feel.

I can feel you here with me . Your presence is so strong. It's beautiful.

Your mannerisms, your smile, your touch, your words are resonating with me and around me.

You are ever present in my heart.

- - - - - - -

Mum,

Today I wrote this:

Wishing everyone a day where love radiates from within.

Today I am being guided every step of the way by my intuition.

- - - - - - -

Mum,

Love has no boundaries. When I focus my intent to connect with you then you are beside me every step of the way. When I am still with you the connection is stronger. Your presence when I sit or walk with you in peaceful places like the garden or by the ocean brings joy to my heart.

Hi Mum,

I remember when I was a child the excitement of opening gifts on my Birthday and at Christmas time. The joy and laughter was exhilarating.

Well I've got that feeling right now. The printer just rang to say my journal 'Mum Moments - Journey Through Grief' is in transit.

Whoopeeeeeeeeeeeee....

The excitement is exhilarating.

I am breathing gently and spending a quiet moment connecting with you and sharing the amazing journey we have been on since your death.

I am crying as I write this. I would still love to be experiencing the joy of you physically opening the boxes with me, hugging me and dancing with joy. This is not to be.

I know you are beside me every step of the way. You are guiding me to take a breath, wrap my precious shawl around me and take some time to be in the moment appreciating the journey I have been on.

You are encouraging me to celebrate the new journey I am about to begin.

I love you Mum.

- - - - - - -

My willingness to experience grief following my mother's death in 2011 has brought me home to a place in my heart where we will live as one forever.

Mum,

I live personal development. I practise walking my talk daily. I help people help themselves.

Self Awareness is the key.

When you are aware of what motivates you then you have a choice every step of the way.

It takes practice, one step at a time.

- - - - - - -

Mum,

As I sit with a copy of my journal, 'Mum Moments - Journey Through Grief' I reflect on one of the saddest days of my life when you died.

Now I celebrate your life by sharing the love and compassion you eloquently expressed in your life through my journal.

The joy I feel in my heart in this moment is phenomenal. This joy goes way beyond the boundaries of life and death and I am grateful to have found this place guided by you, my Mum.

You live in my heart forever.

- - - - - - -

Mum,

In the silence of the moment I celebrate life and death. Love transcends the human experience.

Mum,

Today I wrote:

Take a moment wherever you are to put your hand on your heart and feel your Mother's love. No matter what your experiences with your mother have been or are today, in life and death a mother's love is a powerful force which stays with you forever.

Hi Mum,

Writing this journal has helped and supported me on so many different levels. Observing the way my words have resonated for so many other people who have either lost their mother through death or have felt disconnected from their mother in life has been a humbling experience.

My hope is that 'Mum Moments - Journey Through Grief' will support others on their own personal journey.

Love and light to us all.

Mum,

Sitting on the front porch wishing for you to be sitting beside me.

It's not like the way it was before.

It's different now.

Mum,

Today my Act of Self Love is to be grateful.

I am grateful to my gorgeous husband John. He is my soul mate. Our marriage has been a roller coaster ride with some amazing times and some not so amazing.

He has encouraged and supported me to realise my dream as a writer. He has worked passionately behind the scenes each step of the way.

The best part of all is that this project has strengthened our relationship and shown me how much I value sharing my life with him.

- - - - - - -

Mum,

Imagine if everyone took some time to be still today, whatever that may mean for each one of us.

Some of the ways I find stillness are through meditation, going for a walk, stepping outside into nature, stopping and focusing on my breathing.

I am usually guided by my intuition when to be still.

- - - - - - -

> Yesterday I stepped into fear
> and went for the ride.
>
> Today I observed the fear and
> came home to my heart.

Mum,

I was awake at 4:00am this morning.

I cuddled up warm under the blankets and allowed myself to observe my thoughts without judgement. What an amazing space to be in, allowing the thoughts and feeling peace in my heart. There was no attachment, I felt a smile ... there was joy in my heart.

I hopped out of bed to check a few things. On my return my intuition guided me to pick up a pillow and cuddle it as the child within me.

Wow .. The power of love was amazing. The connection with me was profound.

- - - - - - -

> Today I'm listening to my intuition. I'm in tune with my heart.

- - - - - - -

Mum,

In the middle of the night I didn't want to be sick. My creative juices were stagnant. I was overcome with fears and doubts.

In the morning I have surrendered to being sick. My creative juices are flowing. I feel comfortable and confident.

Resting in bed with a warm honey and lemon drink allowing my mind, body and spirit healing time.

> I love reminders that bring me home to the magnificence of the present moment.

Mum,

Today I am allowing myself to feel all my feelings.

I am practicing observing my feelings without becoming them.

This means I am practicing being aware of my feelings rather than being triggered by the issues they raise in me. I am practicing owning my stuff and letting others own theirs.

I'm doing well today. It's not always easy.

My message to me is I acknowledge my feelings and stay in my HEARTSPACE.

Share the flavours of your Mum. What food does she or did she make for you that you can still taste now?

I can taste the delicious chicken sandwiches my mum often made for celebrations. I can also remember the amazing ribbon sandwiches and so much more ...

What can you remember?

Mum,

Grieving is a deeply personal and poetic experience. I know now that until you experience it you have no idea how it could possibly feel and by that time it's too late.

You are thrown into the depths of despair as you flounder down a new road.

You discover emotions that are hidden away inside of you that often take you completely by surprise and you don't know what to do with them.

I was in this space when you died suddenly in 2011 and in amongst the whirlwind of emotions I started to write and I kept writing as the days, weeks, year and more years rolled by.

I say to people now: 'Writing gave me the perfect tool to grieve and survive the deep emotions that surfaced, allowing me to connect with the beautiful memories of my mother and find a new way to connect with her where she will always have a special place in my heart.'

Love you.

- - - - - - -

Mum,

You always provided delicious scrumptious food for everyone. There are so many wonderful memories that I can still taste when I imagine the meals you cooked.

Your chicken broth when I was sick holds a special place in my heart ... the warm lamb and corn fritters you walked with up to school on a cold winter's day at lunchtime ... your scones with jam and cream ... your delightful chicken sandwiches ... and so much more.

There's nothing as good as your own mum's cooking.

- - - - - - -

Mum,

It saddens me on a deep level the separation in some families.

There are so many perceptions and misunderstandings that have occurred throughout everyone's lives.

We all have our own versions and it is easy to stick with our version, our pain, our hurt, our belief of how it is and who can we blame.

Another option is to own our own stuff. Acknowledge we have all fought, argued, disagreed , perceived, and misunderstood.

Everyone has the choice to continue exactly as they are choosing, to mix with those in their family who do it their way and separate from those who don't.

Alternatively we can all come from a place in our hearts where we acknowledge the pain and hurt we feel and then make a choice to choose love and compassion as a way to heal.

We are all brothers and sisters ... mothers and fathers ... sons and daughters ...

- - - - - - -

Mum,

Today I wrote:

'As Mother's Day approaches celebrate your own special mum, celebrate being a Mum and all this means to you.

Please take a moment to feel some compassion for all the people who have lost their mothers through death or other circumstances.

Mother's Day is never the same after loss.

If you know someone whose mother is no longer present you may like to offer them a hug in recognition of their mum.

I believe stepping outside your comfort zone and saying 'I'm sorry for your loss, I don't know what to say', is better than not saying anything.

Share some love and compassion.'

- - - - - - -

Mum,

I am practicing delayed gratification today.

My heart is peaceful as I observe and respond to my challenges.

The more I practise observing and responding as an alternative to reacting, the better it gets.

- - - - - - -

Mum,

As I sit quietly in my room before bed I look around at all the things you gave to me.

Exquisite notebooks too beautiful to write in ...

My warm and cuddly shawl...

The books by authors we both love: Maeve Binchy, Marian Keyes and Monica McInerney ...

I love these moments ... the stillness where I feel your presence.

It's hard to comprehend you are dead when you feel ever present in my life.

Our love has no boundaries.

I love you Mum

- - - - - - -

Mum,

As I reflect on the cold autumn day I remember your Sunday roasts and the delicious creations you then made for dinner from the left overs. I can taste them as I write.

Curled up by the open fire on a cold winter's night watching New Faces on TV was a favourite for me in the 70's.

On facebook I often ask: 'What is your memory on a cold winter's night with your mum?'

Mum,

I have just been to an open mic night for women where women share their stories. I am deeply touched by these courageous people who are willing to be vulnerable. There was laughter and tears and so much more and I am grateful I was able to share excerpts from my book.

- - - - - - -

Tears are a beautiful place to feel.

Tears heal.

- - - - - - -

Hi Mum,

Mother's Day approaches. Here come the emotions.

That's what happens when you are a mother. That's what happens when you are a child.

From the moment of conception the mother child connection is there forever.

- - - - - - -

Mum,

Today I was in the kitchen and I felt like I was you. I was preparing some food in the kitchen. Wow it was amazing.

- - - - - - -

Mum,

I miss your physical presence in my life however I know you are right beside me every step of the way.

I will be celebrating the importance of mothers at my book launch and on Mother's Day.

I will feel my emotions in any given moment to celebrate who I am.

I am grateful to you for all the lessons I have learnt on this amazing journey.

- - - - - - -

Mum,

Today I wrote:

'Just after my mum died a friend of hers took me to a cafe they had enjoyed together. There were tears and laughter as we shared all that mum was to us both. We could feel her energy, it was beautiful. I have returned there several times to feel her presence.

Today I visited this cafe again with my husband. As my fourth Mother's Day since mum died approaches her spiritual essence is shining and I felt her presence with us. These experiences bring joy to my heart.

I am grateful for the wonderful cafes and shops around Melbourne where her energy radiates.'

Love you Mum.

- - - - - - -

Mum,

Sometimes I just need to stop, slow down and take a breath. I'm doing it now.

- - - - - - -

Hi Mum,

I feel the sparkle of your smile in the sunshine.

Love you

- - - - - - -

Mum,

I'm feeling peaceful.

Today I launch my book. It's my journal where I allowed myself to experience the emotions of grief and celebrate you and the influence you had on my life and continue to have today.

Whenever I write it still feels like you are here with me, loving and supporting me every step of the way.

I love you mum. You inspire me.

- - - - - - -

Mum,

I'm feeling exhausted and unbelievably emotional tonight. The tears are flowing freely. It's been an amazing week for me.

I launched my 'Mum Moments' book on Friday night.

I launched my Facebook page with the same name and our website where I was ready to share who I am with the world.

I am overwhelmed with already over 400 likes on my page. People are buying my journal face to face, on Amazon and on our website.

My heart has been touched with comments and sharing from around the world from people who are grieving for lost loved ones.

- - - - - - -

Mum,

Allowing my emotions to flow on Mother's Day. Tears and laughter. The empty feeling in my heart and stomach. Massaging my stomach with my hand on my heart as I feel the love

Sharing time with my family. Missing your physical presence in my life. Valuing my spiritual connection with you.

My daughter took me to the Mother's Day walk in the city. 40,000 people running or walking to celebrate mothers. The sun shone as we talked and walked.

Brunch with the kids.

Looking forward to sharing time with John when he gets home from work.

The journey has been a roller coaster and I am so happy I have found a way to come home to my heart.

A candle has been burning brightly in my home today as a recognition of mothers everywhere.

It's my fourth Mother's Day today since you died and has been filled with joy, laughter and tears.

I am so grateful for my family who bring so much joy into my life.

- - - - - - -

I write to my mum, I talk to her, I feel her everywhere.

I cry, I laugh, I live.

I am surrounded by her love.

My mum lives in my heart forever.

- - - - - - -

Mum,

I am sitting peacefully by the heater with a candle burning brightly for you and everyone else's mother.

In the moments I am still I feel your presence. The moment is precious.

This moment is the essence of my connection with you, my mum.

- - - - - - -

When I allow myself some time
to be still I find a way to
connect with you in my heart
space.

- - - - - - -

Mum,

It's like a new day, a new way and it takes practise to adjust. Practise to find a new way of living, a new way of connecting.

Remember, death does not take away the connection. Death separates us from the physical however we are connected in our hearts forever.

- - - - - - -

I find my mum in Nature.

- - - - - - -

Mum,

My intuition is guiding me.

My ego is screaming.

My intuition is speaking gently to my ego, acknowledging my ego's purpose and discovering a new bond.

- - - - - - -

Mum,

Today is 'Challenge Day' with a Facebook group I am with.

My day started feeling challenged. I was feeling like I needed to make it happen, now.

I allowed my intuition to guide me. I stopped, I meditated, I went for a walk.

I saw this flower peeping through the fence. It reminded me it is possible to find a way through.

- - - - - - -

Observing my fears.

Aware of my ego.

Being guided by my intuition.

- - - - - - -

Mum,

Fear has hit me.

I'm scared.

I don't know where to go or what to do.

I've created something very special, something that is me. It is my own self-expression and I've put it out there.

I feel I need to go inside myself and find the heart and soul of what is happening for me. To open my heart to the people who need it.

I know my journal has the power to offer love, comfort and support to so many. So I remember to believe in myself just like you always believed in me.

I need to take the steps so it can all unfold.

Mum,

I visit the cemetery occasionally where your ashes are buried.

I feel your presence wherever I am.

I feel you right beside me.

I have favourite places where you loved to go and I go there for extra comfort and connection.

Jude

Mum,

Listening to my intuition.

This morning: meditation, writing, stillness, writing, meditation, writing ...

Connecting to my inner knowing, connecting to the gifts I have been presented with to share the love that is the essence of who we are.

My heart is radiating.

May everyone feel Radiance wherever they are.

Mum,

I like to share the things I've learnt. I'm an intuitive and I know I'm being guided every step of the way. I have a choice to listen and follow the guidance and I have a choice to ignore the guidance and choose another direction.

Whatever I choose is perfect in that particular moment.

We are all intuitive. We are all born intuitive.

It's really very simple. We get yes feelings and we get no feelings.

We know in our heart the answer for us right now.

If my words resonate for you then please practise listening to your intuition and discover the power of love that radiates from within you.

- - - - - - -

Hi Mum,

I feel so at home with you now. It's different ... it works for me ... it works for you ...

I can feel it.

I sit in the garden. I can feel you in my words. I can feel you in the breeze. I can feel you everywhere.

Our love resides in my heart and it is beautiful.

- - - - - - -

Mum,

I've been an intuitive all my life. I know I am loved and supported by the Higher Source within us all.

I know I have been guided every step of the way throughout my life.

Sometimes I've listened and sometimes I've lived the human experience of 'this is how you do it ... this is what you should do ... this is the way it is'.

This human experience can be difficult and I have at times felt complete resistance to this feeling of 'the majority rules'.

I felt the radiance of me in my heart so many times in my life but then allowed others' perceptions of 'how it is' overtake my own feelings. Sometimes it is easier to simply 'go with the flow'.

Now my heart is radiating and it's time for the radiance within to shine outwards and for me to share the experience of living with Love in the world.

This is not about changing the world ... this is about me seeking the essence of Love in the heart and soul of every person who crosses my path.

The positive and negative experiences that present in life are all part of living from our HEARTSPACE and knowing all is well.

Here's my ego saying: 'what are you talking about? I don't get what you are saying at all. How can you find love in the pain and suffering? Nah, this bit doesn't resonate for me at all. See you can't give me an answer to this one can you?'

I say: 'go and find stillness and feel this one ... feel the answers.

Today I am radiating love from my heart to everyone who I am having or have ever had a relationship with in my life. Your presence in my life is a gift however it presents. It helps bring me home to my heart.

My ego is again saying 'I'm still not sure it's the answer'.

I say: Ego, let's sit with it for a while. Be still with my heart and feel the beauty we are.

- - - - - - -

Mum,

This morning I went for a walk, feeling like I was in a tug of war with myself. In my mind I called out to you, 'I'm stuck, what now'?

In that moment my intuition said lie down in the grass now. I was resistant and then I lay down.

A broken branch presented as I enjoyed the feeling of the breeze. You often collected branches that had fallen when you were out walking.

I picked up the branch and there was a feeling of calm ... to be still ... that everything was okay.

I know there are signs in every experience. You shared this message with me during your life and your guidance continues to support me now.

I love you mum

Hi Mum,

Feeling a bit like I'm in a tug of war again. My intuition is guiding me, my ego is pulling me in the other direction.

I'm feeling the pull. I'm walking with it, aware of it and observing it.

In the past this tug of war has manifested with a feeling presenting as a huge hole in my solar plexus.

Right now my solar plexus feels balanced with all my chakras.

This is a positive step for me.

- - - - - - -

Mum,

Today I thought:

'I'm in a good space right now. My heart is radiating.'

I'm sending love and hugs out to everyone.

- - - - - - -

I find experiencing all my emotions without judging myself helps me and brings me home into my heart.

Writing has helped me so much. When the emotions are raw I just write them till I come out the other side.

When the emotions feel good I write them too.

- - - - - - -

I would like to acknowledge all Mothers, Mums, Moms, Mamas, Mams and others who embrace the role be it surrogate, step or foster.

Mum, I loved making daisy chains with you when I was a child. It still brings a smile to my face today.

Hi Mum,

Feelings are who I am and I'm okay.

When I'm sad I feel sad. When I'm lonely I feel lonely. When I'm happy I feel happy. When I'm glad I feel glad.

There is no right or wrong when it comes to feelings.

I practise feeling my feelings in any given moment. When I do this the feelings come and go. If I try to block my feelings, push them away, then they hold tight and I feel sick. I shut down and I die inside while I function in the world.

Today I live as me. I feel … and I give myself permission to feel *all* my feelings without judgement.

The more I allow my feelings, the more I feel at home with the joy in my heart.

Mum,

This is what I wrote today:

'I just lit a candle for me, for you, for your loved ones.

Today I practise feeling my feelings. Today I embrace all my feelings. It is okay to be me.'

'Sometimes I light a candle. It helps me.'

Mum,

When I play music and sing along to songs you and I loved it brings up the emotions. Sometimes I sing songs from my childhood like the 'Sound of Music' at the top of my voice and I can feel you singing with me.

Today I plant seeds of hope

Hi Mum,

When I go to sleep tonight I'm going to grab a pillow and hug it and imagine hugging you, feeling your hug and feeling the love we have that lives in our hearts forever.

I will also imagine sending hugs to everyone who is experiencing grief around the world.

Mum,

You gave me Ronan Keatings CD, 'Songs For My Mother' for Christmas in 2010.

You died suddenly in February 2011.

I have played this CD so many times. It has supported me through the pain and sorrow of your loss and has helped me stay connected with you in our own special way.

To me, your Angels were preparing us for this life changing event.

I love you mum. You are always with me.

- - - - - - - -

Mum,

I have found ways to connect with you since you died because that's what's happened.

Yes I want you here, I want you now and if that was possible that's exactly how I would have it.

That is not how it is. Death changes everything. You are not here physically in my life and it sucks.

I can sit in the sucks as much as I like. I can drown in the sucks and be completely overwhelmed.

I've felt every feeling conceivable and allowed them to flow. At times I resisted and the pain in my head took over my body.

As soon as I allowed the feelings to flow, observed them and gave them permission to surface then the pain in my body disappeared.

When I feel I am in tune with me I provide a space for self expression and healing.

In this space I have found healing tools that work for me and I can feel you in any given moment of every day.

Feeling is where healing begins.

- - - - - - -

Hi Mum,

My words today:

'Yes if it was possible I would like my mum with me here right now so I could hug her tight and tell her I love her.

No, it's not possible because she is dead.

So instead I walk with her by my side in spirit.

I observe her presence in my surroundings and I feel the essence of her in my heart.

This gives me comfort.'

Love you mum

- - - - - - -

Are you resisting your grieving emotions?

It is okay to grieve.

It is okay to feel.

- - - - - - -

Mum,

Sometimes there are no words so I'm sitting here thinking about you with my hand on my heart.

- - - - - - -

Mum,

Feeling is an important part of grieving. Allowing the raw and 'painful' feelings helps them flow and makes room for the 'good' stuff.

- - - - - - -

Mum,

I wrote this today:

'Live in the moment.

The precious moments stay in your heart forever.

Fill your heart with moments.'

- - - - - - -

Mum,

Today I wrote about you ...

'My mum touched hearts.'

- - - - - - -

Mum,

Through my writing I feel I am following a tradition.

Now I say: 'If my words resonate, hold them in your heart and feel the love within you.'

Love you Mum

- - - - - - -

Mum,

With my 'Mum Moments – Journey Through Grief' book it's 'one with the lot'.

You get all the emotions and feelings combined with love and support.

- - - - - - -

Mum,

We are all beautiful beings. Getting to know ourselves and loving all of us brings us home to our hearts.

It helps me. I practise unconditional love of myself daily which represents the same unconditional love you gave me. It's a warts and all package. lol ...

Hi Mum,

Hand on my heart for me, hand on my heart for you and sending love and compassion all around the world for all those who need to feel the love.

I am grateful for all the tools you gave me in life to connect with you. They continue after your death, too.

- - - - - - -

Mum,

I wrote this today. I'm hoping it might help:

'Sharing, caring, feeling is so important. The numb, the raw, the sobbing, the 'it's not fair', the pain.

The feeling that it's not real, that my mum is going to walk up the driveway, that she'll give me a call.

The reality.

These are some of the many and more emotions you may be feeling in the early days. There is no right or wrong. It is what it is.

I'm more than 3 years down the track from my mum's death. Writing all my feelings down along with the many other steps I have taken - including experiencing all the above feelings - has helped me to find ways to stay connected with my mum.

I still miss her physical presence in my life and oh, how I'd love it to be as it was when she was alive.

It's different now, I still feel her in my life every day.'

My Act of Self Love today was expressing my feelings.

Mum,

Today I went to the hospital where you died 3 years and 3 months ago.

I told them that when you died no one said to me that there was any support available.

I made them aware that even if they tell something to the next of kin - being my father in this instance - that does not mean the rest of the family knows.

When someone dies everyone is in shock and hospitals need to make sure everyone in a family knows what type of support is available.

Families are complex and next of kin may be so caught up in their own stuff that they may not even consider other family members and their needs.

In my experience grief takes you completely by surprise no matter what your belief system is.

Mum, I am on my own journey through grief which continues to surprise me. I still miss your physical presence in my life. I feel totally connected to you on a spiritual level and I feel you with me every day.

I am grateful that the intensive Care Unit and the Social Work Department appreciated the need to make all family members aware in the future that support is available.

My Mum died ... it sucks ... what now?

- - - - - - -

Mum,

I've had one of 'those' days and this is what I wrote:

'Grief - what's that?

I've got no idea. It's numb it hurts. I don't want to feel. I don't care. It hurts.

I want my mummy.

It sucks, it's not fair.

Look at all those old people when my mum is dead and they are alive. My mum was such a young 78 it's not fair.

I miss her I want her she's gone. It's not fair.

What next?

Where do I go?

What do I do?

How, why, when?'

- - - - - - -

Mum,

I'm feeling stuck in all the 'have to's ...

I'm feeling overwhelmed with the nitty gritty. The stuff keeps building. The stuff stops me from doing the real stuff I want to do because there's always so much stuff.

The list that's getting left behind overwhelms me.

The stuff that gets too much is holding me back. I need to shift it. I need to move through it and open the door.

It's time ...

- - - - - - -

Mum,

Moment by moment today.

Dad had another heart attack last night. He is stable.

Sometimes I wonder about the medical profession and how many drugs they pump into elderly people and all the technology.

Allowing myself to experience all my emotions in motion.

Accepting me and allowing all my thoughts are okay.

- - - - - - -

Today I practise random acts of kindness.

Mum,

Right now I need a hug.

I'm happy to give and receive hugs.

I just closed my eyes and hugged a pillow and allowed myself to have visions of those I was hugging. It was beautiful.

I find hugging a wonderful way to experience my emotions.

- - - - - - -

Mum,

Compassion is my lesson at the moment.

People who always present as strong are often hiding their vulnerability. Those that present as vulnerable are often hiding their strength.

Loving all aspects of myself and being myself allows me to have compassion for others.

Love you

- - - - - - -

Mum,

Dad had another heart attack yesterday. His condition is stable.

I'm sitting with my emotions as I reflect on the complexities of life.

As I sat and held his hand yesterday there were so many different emotions.

I asked you for advice and you reminded me of what I said when I held your hand before you died: 'choose what's best for you'.

Just for the moment I could do with a hug.

- - - - - - -

Hi Mum,

I'm going for a walk right now.

I love these moments.

I love the surprises when I take time to walk and feel your presence right beside me.

- - - - - - -

Mum,

Grief took me completely by surprise when you died suddenly. It's a roller coaster of emotions. The emotions come and go.

I know now there is no right or wrong on this journey. Sometimes I will feel okay, sometimes I will feel I am not coping.

I say to everyone, 'Do your best to love and nurture yourself.'

I found writing my feelings was a great way to express myself and move through.

Mum,

These words came today:

'STOP for a moment. Be still with yourself. Breathe in, breathe out and then do it again.

Ask yourself, 'What is the best thing I can do for myself right now?'

You will have your answer before you have finished the question.

You know what is best for you.'

> Grieving has its raw moments and grieving has the special moments. I take the moments as they come.

Mum,

When I feel hurt, I bring the hurt into my heart and allow the hurt to be there as I surround the hurt with love.

I know it will pass when it is ready.

Hi Mum,

I opened the curtains this morning to fog outside the window and was uplifted by the sunshine I could see coming through behind it.

When we are grieving we can get lost in the fog. It's always good to remember the sunshine will warm its way through.

- - - - - - -

Mum,

Today a friend of a friend lost her mum. It takes me back to when you died.

I realise that sometimes there are no words you can say, no words that can possibly come close to the reality of the death of a loved one.

So tonight I light a candle for those beginning the grieving journey and those already experiencing it.

- - - - - - -

Wounds hurt and wounds heal
when we feel the pain.

- - - - - - -

Mum,

Embracing me today ...

I come as one with the lot ... Emotions in motion.

Hi Mum,

I'm sitting in my human-ness. Some of it is comfortable, some not.

I feel best when I operate from my heart but there are times when my ego steps in.

- - - - - - -

Mum,

You know those moments when you're feeling down, those moments when a 'Mum Hug' is just what you need? I'm having one of those moments now.

Hugs to anyone having one of those moments.

- - - - - - -

Mum,

Sharing helps you and helps others too.

I know my life with you had highs, lows and in-betweens, and I know all those experiences strengthened our relationship.

- - - - - - -

> I cannot remove the hurt and pain for they are a part of grieving

Mum,

I say to my clients:

'I'm here to help you express yourself.

I'm here to help you tune into your intuition for guidance so you can make choices in your life that resonate for you.'

Helping people empower themselves feels amazing. I am so thankful.

> When I experience my HEARTSPACE, wherever I am, whatever is happening, I feel truly blessed.

Mum,

I practise knowing myself and healing myself.

I help others practise knowing themselves and healing themselves.

In the stillness we get to know ourselves, listen to ourselves and make choices in our life that truly resonate with our heart.

This takes practise.

The more we practise the more we understand ourselves. At this point we have the opportunity to observe what motivates us in every aspect of our life and make choices that resonate with our true self.

I live this way. I love this way. My heart radiates from a space of love living this way.

I am human so I too slip out of my heart space. I see this as a positive sign to remind me of what is important in my life.

When we are ready we can step into our heart space more often. Everything begins when we are ready.

- - - - - - -

Mum, who am I with all this?

'You are a kind and considerate person who loves helping others. Help yourself first and the rest will follow?'

So what does that mean?

'You take the steps first. You discover how it helps others and then you guide others to help themselves.

You do not fix anyone ... you help others find tools to help themselves.'

It sounds simple.

'It sounds simple for you. It is not simple for others. They need to learn to listen to their inner voices which can take time and practise.

You have been aware of your inner voices most of your life.

Sometimes you have listened, sometimes you have not.

Now you are listening to your inner voices most of the time. However you slip in and out of this. You are human and that is alright.

You need to keep practising this as your life will be fulfilled by living this truth,

You will help so many people by speaking out, by being real and helping them to be real too.

The love that will abound will be amazing beyond anything you have ever believed.

Just keep doing it. You are on the right track and you are beautiful, bountiful and blissful.

Thank you for listening

Love love love that is all.'

- - - - - - -

> Stress happens. You can
> observe it or become it.

- - - - - - -

Mum,

I am humbled by the connections I make when I open my heart.

- - - - - - -

Mum,

Last night I enjoyed dinner and a movie with my family.

Sitting in the foyer waiting for them at the end of the movie, I observed an elderly couple walking out of the cinema and had one of those moments where I feel 'it's hard to believe my mum is not here'.

I can see you so clearly and feel you so clearly … you are forever young in my heart.

- - - - - - -

There's a time for silence and a time for sharing.

Which do you need right now?

- - - - - - -

Mum,

I'm practicing what I believe daily. My intuition is radiating and my ego is screaming to be heard.

Most of the time I'm gently guiding my ego home to my Heartspace. Sometimes my ego is taking over. At these times I'm embracing my emotions and find a way back to my HEARTSPACE.

- - - - - - -

Mum,

This morning I embraced my tears and found my heart.

Hi Mum,

I'm having one of those days where I'm feeling vulnerable. I'm embracing it rather than resisting it.

I'm about to go for a walk, feel my feelings and take my day moment by moment.

- - - - - - -

Take a moment.

Practice allowing your feelings.

Find a quiet place.

Close your eyes.

Breathe gently.

Observe your thoughts.

Observe your body and how it feels.

Put your hand on your heart.

Be still for a while.

Practice this and discover the healing power within you.

This works for me.

- - - - - - -

> Nurturing yourself ... knowing yourself ... making positive choices for yourself

Mum,

Sometimes I need to sit back and observe my feelings. My feelings have a purpose and sometimes I see the purpose of my feelings clearly.

Other times I have no idea what the purpose is so I sit, breathe and observe. In the stillness I ask 'what can I do right now?'

The answer is clear before I finish the question.

- - - - - - -

Mum,

I'm sitting quietly, patting my dog, thinking about you, and that one of the best things I ever learnt from you was compassion.

Thank you.

- - - - - - -

Mum,

I'm lying in bed, quiet background music, breathing gently, feeling love in it purest form.

I am radiating love to everyone and it feels amazing.

- - - - - - -

Mum,

Sometimes I hug a pillow and I can feel the warmth of your hugs.

Sometimes I have no idea, and
that's ok with me.

- - - - - - -

Mum,

Emotions come and go ... seasons come and go.

My experience of grieving has been like the seasons.

Seasons come and seasons go.

Sometimes there is rain ... sometimes sunshine.

A massive storm erupts and then it's gone.

Light rain gently falls day after day and then it clears.

Grieving comes ... grieving goes.

Seasons come... seasons go.

Sometimes there is rain ... sometimes there is sunshine.

Massive storms erupt and then they go.

Light rain falls day after day and then it clears.

The clouds they come and go ...

The sun always shines through.

- - - - - - -

Mum,

A powerful weekend.

Living in the moment, intuitively guided every step of the way. Felt empowered and in tune.

Overnight I woke up in the early hours of this morning. Fear, doubt, guilt presented. I embraced it, I faced it, I was in it.

I was uncomfortable. I didn't know what to do with it so I let it be.

Eventually slept for a while then woke to 'I'm not doing that anymore.'

Slept peacefully knowing I'm on the perfect pathway for me.

- - - - - - -

Mum,

You are a special part of my life. I live with you by my side every day. Your love radiates in all that I do. Your love has no boundaries.

Death may have removed your physical presence but your power to connect with me has opened my heart and soul to amazing experiences beyond life as I know it. It's different now.

I have a beautiful relationship with you now because I have embraced it as it is.

All that we shared in life I share with you now. I talk to you. I listen to you. I question you. I love you. It is truly beautiful. Our communication is so clear.

It's like the human interpretation has been removed and every conversation has clarity and compassion. All that often got in the way of understanding in life is gone. We hear each other. We understand each other and there is no confusion in the messages we share. It is amazing.

I love it ... in many ways it is even better than it was before.

- - - - - - -

Mum, today I wrote:

I've shared some special moments with my mum in the silence of the morning.

How do you connect with your mum or loved one each day?

- - - - - - -

Hand on your heart, hold on, embrace all your feelings.

Observe your feelings, express your feelings.

Every feeling I know surfaced after my mum's death. Many feelings took me completely by surprise.

I shut down, I opened up.

I wrote to express my feelings. The more I wrote, the more I connected. The more I connected, the more I developed a new relationship with my mum. It's different now and its beautiful.

I held on, I embraced grief. I found my way home to my heart.

I talk to my mum everyday. She talks to me too. We support each other on a different journey.

I am so grateful for my mum.

- - - - - - -

HEARTSPACE

Dedicated to my Mum whose light continues to shine everywhere.

Celebrating my family John, Jack and Noni who bring joy to my heart.

Thank you John Taylor for being my husband, soulmate and greatest supporter as we navigate through this adventure called life.

To my children Jack and Noni, thank you for being you and shining your own unique light on the world.

Lynda Cheldelin Fell, Glen Lord, Rose Inserra, Alison Burton and Angela Cartwright, I am inspired by the way you dedicate your lives to helping and supporting others. I appreciate the love, understanding and kindness that you share with me on my own journey. Our connection is beautiful even though some of us live on opposite sides of the world.

Since launching my first book 'MUM MOMENTS - Journey Through Grief' in 2014 my friendship circles have grown and now span the continents of our world. I know I simply cannot name you all ... instead I am putting my hand on my heart and radiating love and a special 'thank you' to you.

Jude xoxoxo

Also by JudyTaylor
'MUM MOMENTS
Journey Through Grief'

2014

ISBN: 978-0-9924900-0-3

www.ingramcontent.com/pod-product-compliance
Lightning Source LLC
Chambersburg PA
CBHW070542300426
44113CB00011B/1755